Visualize Your Message
Turning Intangibles into Effective Communication

Table of Contents

Chapter 1. Introduction

In a bustling world where everyone is inundated with endless streams of information, how can you ensure your message stands out? Welcome to our thrilling Special Report, "Visualize Your Message: Turning Intangibles into Effective Communication"! This delightful, easy-to-grasp guide throws open the door to a space where creativity meets comprehension, offering hands-on strategies to enhance your communication skills. You'll discover methods to transform abstract concepts into visual ones, captivating your audience every time they look at your infographic, presentation, or social media post. Who knew turning intangibles into effective communication could be so seamless and enjoyable? Make your words leave an indelible visual imprint – let's get started!

Chapter 2. Understanding Visual Communication

At the intersection of imagery and narrative lies the powerful tool known as visual communication. This potent communication style utilizes design elements and visual aids to express information, ideas, and concepts, making them more digestible and engaging than other forms of media. Captivating the audience's attention in a sea of textual content, visual communication is a necessary component in today's fast-paced and information-dense landscape.

2.1. The Definition and Scope of Visual Communication

Visual communication entails using visual aids to convey, express, or communicate an idea, thought, concept, or information. The visual cues employed could range from images, graphics, signs, designs to symbols, drawings, charts, diagrams – the list could go on. Stepping out from the constraints of text-only communication, visual communication adds a graphical element making your message multidimensional and more engaging. It could even encompass multimedia scenarios where visual elements team up with auditory ones, such as videos, animations, and interactive presentations.

The wonder of visual communication does not stop at its ability to captivate attention but extends to its talent in aiding comprehension. According to the Picture Superiority Effect, people have a better recall of information presented visually. Hence, visual communication can make a lasting impression, facilitating better understanding and retention.

2.2. Visual Communication and Its Effect on Our Brain

The human brain has a natural inclination towards visual information. Multiple studies have shown that when paired with text, visuals lead to a significant improvement in information retention. This phenomenon is grounded in the dual-coding theory, implying that our brains process visual and verbal information simultaneously but in separate channels. When we pair information from both channels, we create a more robust memory trace.

Visual communication also leverages our brain's ability to comprehend details from patterns and structures. The mind deciphers images faster than text because we can perceive whole images all at once while texts need to be processed sequentially.

Moreover, emotions have a crucial role in decision making, and visual cues can evoke strong emotional responses. Images can trigger feelings, actions, and even behavioural changes faster and more effectively than words can.

2.3. Components of Visual Communication

Visual communication is not a random collection of images or graphics. It involves the strategic use of elements that can be categorized into the following:

1. Images: These could be photographs, illustrations, or icons that best represent the message you are trying to portray. The right image can strengthen your narrative and make it easier for your audience to understand.

2. Color: It's not just about making your visual communication more appealing but also involves triggering specific emotions or

reactions. Each color has a psychological interpretation that can influence your audience's perception and reaction.

3. Lines and Shapes: These elements define boundaries within your visual communication, guiding the viewer's eye and highlighting specific information. They can be used to create division, emphasis and harmony within the design.

4. Typography: This involves the style, arrangement, and appearance of text within your visual communication. The right font and style can set the tone, create an atmosphere, and even evoke specific emotions.

5. Layout: The arrangement and organization of elements on a page is essential. A cluttered layout can confuse your audience, while a well-organized one can guide their attention to the most crucial parts of the message.

2.4. The Power of Infographics in Visual Communication

Infographics, a blend of graphs, charts, images, and minimal text, are a quintessential example of visual communication. They are a popular tool due to their power to simplify complex information and translate it into a visually engaging format that is quick to understand and easy to remember.

Infographics play on the strengths of both textual and visual communication. Textual elements provide the context, while visuals create an immediate impression on the viewers. Together, they make data and facts easier to comprehend.

2.5. Polishing Your Visual Communication Skills

Visual communication does not require you to be a natural-born artist or designer. There are plenty of resources and software available that can aid in creating engaging visuals provided you understand your audience, your medium, and your message. However, refining your skills certainly involves being aware of design principles, appreciating the power of space and balance, understanding how to use contrast and colors, tackling textual elements, and making data visually pleasing.

To get better at visual communication skills, consume varied types of visual content and pay attention to what captures your attention and why. The practice of understanding what makes an infographic, for example, easy or difficult to understand can help build your acumen. Experimenting with different tools and applications can also expand your knowledge.

To sum it up, visual communication skills are becoming increasingly important in all walks of life - whether it's in professional settings for presentations and reports, in marketing and advertising, or even for personal social media use. Becoming proficient in this language of visuals not only makes your messages impactful but also gives them a compelling factor in a world overflowing with words.

Chapter 3. The Power of Infographics

We live in an era frequently referred to as the age of information. Today, numerous media outlets and the internet bombard us with continual streams of data. Yet, amid this deluge, a tool has emerged to highlight crucial information and whisk it to the forefront with panache - Infographics.

Infographics, graphics that display information, have emerged as powerful vehicles to communicate complex data in a visually appealing and easy-to-understand format. Not only do they break down intricate information into digestible segments, but they also enhance cognitive recall, fitting in beautifully with our predominantly visual culture.

3.1. Why Infographics?

Our brains process visual content significantly faster than textual content. According to a MIT study, we can comprehend an image in just 13 milliseconds. This is partly due to our evolutionary history: Western Lowland Gorillas spend nearly 45% of their daytime hours processing visual information – primarily to identify predators and food sources. Not surprisingly, we humans, who share 98% of our DNA with these gentle giants, also have innate preferences for visual information.

Infographics cater to this preference in spades. The combination of imagery, colors, movement, and spatial arrangements amplifies the retention and understanding of information. Furthermore, in our time-crunched society, infographics serve as bite-sized synopses of otherwise bulky information, enabling viewers to grasp main messages at a glance.

3.2. When to Use Infographics?

Given their characteristics, infographics are ideal when you need to: * Demonstrate patterns or trends * Simplify complex data * Present multifaceted research findings * Tell a story or convey an idea with numerical information * Stir interest and engagement in your content

Whether it's in a corporate presentation, an academic report, or a social media post, infographics can propel your message into the limelight.

3.3. Creating Effective Infographics

An effective infographic is more than just a cluster of pictures and words. It requires thoughtful blending of design, facts, and narrative. Here are some tips to create meaningful infographics.

1. Have a Clear Objective: What do you want your audience to understand? Having a clear goal provides your infographic with focus and direction.

2. Collect Reliable Data: The quality of an infographic is directly proportional to the quality of data it houses. Make sure you use credible, up-to-date sources.

3. Create a Flow: A well-structured infographic guides viewers' eyes from one point to another effortlessly. Construct a visual hierarchy - start from the key point and unfold the story step by step.

4. Keep it Simple: Avoid overcrowding your infographic with too many details. Stick to one main idea and a few supporting elements.

5. Quality Over Quantity: A limited number of well-designed, crisp graphics outperform a barrage of cluttered, mediocre visuals

anytime.

6. Colors Matter: Pick a palette that aligns with your message and draws attention. Colors can enhance or inhibit information absorption.

3.4. How to Measure Success?

Quantifying the success of your infographic can be tricky but not impossible. The measurement metrics depend on your initial objective. If the aim was to increase website traffic, keep a tab on click-through rates. Increased shares or likes might indicate success if the goal was expanding social media presence. On the other hand, enhanced understanding or sparked conversations among the audience might be the success indicators for an educational infographic.

Believe it or not, infographics have the potential to revolutionize the way you communicate your ideas. They demand minimal effort from the audience while offering maximum comprehension - a perfect balance in today's age of information overload. So, the next time you find yourself battling to make your message stand out, remember the power of the infographic. Be it capturing attention or enhancing understanding - infographics are the key to effective communication.

Chapter 4. Decoding Abstract Concepts

Grasping abstract concepts isn't always a piece of cake. But the beauty of it resides in the immense potential that these concepts offer when decoded and transformed into a compelling visual representation which simplifies understanding and bolsters recall. Let's sail into this journey of decoding abstract concepts and mastering their visualization!

4.1. What are Abstract Concepts?

In a nutshell, abstract concepts are those which aren't ordinarily perceived through our five senses. They refer to ideas, theories, feelings, or high-level thought processes that are nebulous and elusive, without tangible, physical equivalents. Love, leadership, motivation, psychology, ethics – these all are instances of abstract concepts.

Our greatest challenge, and indeed our greatest opportunity, lies in translating these abstract ideas into communicable, creative visuals that foster impact and engagement.

4.2. Understanding the Challenge

Every coin has two sides and dealing with abstract concepts is no different. These have their own set of complexities. They are often layered, multifaceted, and open to numerous interpretations. How, for instance, would you visually capture 'happiness'? One person might visualize it as a sunny beach, another as a family dinner, and a third person might think of a book-filled room.

This subjective nature of abstract concepts can make identifying a universal depiction quite tricky. Successful communication thus calls for an understanding of your specific target audience, their perspectives, their preferences, and their language.

4.3. Dismantling Abstract Concepts

If abstract concepts are like puzzles, then we need to break them down into smaller, more manageable parts. Once the concept is divided into its essence or key components, you can focus on these separate elements, eventually piecing them together to present a comprehensive whole.

Just like a chef first preparing individual ingredients before combining them into a gourmet dish, we approach complex concepts piece by piece. This stripping down and rebuilding help in raising a concept from the abstract plane to sensible reality.

4.4. Emotion and Symbolism in Visualization

While dealing with intangibles, it's beneficial to appeal to the abstract faculties within your viewers – their emotions. By activating an emotional response, you can trigger empathy, forge a connection and prompt deeper engagement with your content.

But how to evoke emotions visually? Symbols, metaphors, analogies - these are your ready tools. They are deeply ingrained in our collective consciousness and have a powerful effect on our thoughts and emotions. Think about common symbols – a heart to denote love, a light bulb for an idea, or a handshake for agreement. By leveraging these symbols, you can bridge the gap between the abstract concept and the tangible world.

4.5. Color Psychology

Color is another crucial tool to infuse emotion into your visuals. Different colors trigger different responses. For example, red often embodies passion or urgency while blue signifies trust and calmness. Green can convey growth or environment. Familiarizing with color psychology can help construct a palette that resonates with the tonality of your concept.

4.6. Size and Space

How you play with size and space also reflects your message. A larger element portrays significance or dominance. Contrastingly, a smaller one suggests lesser importance or subservience. Similarly, white space or negative space can reflect simplicity, freedom, or even isolation. This basic understanding of size and space can greatly elevate your visual narrative.

4.7. Encapsulating Concepts in a Story

People love stories. They're wired to connect with narratives – hence the success of books, movies, and TV shows. By formulating your abstract concepts into relatable stories, you can make your message more engaging and memorable. It can be an evolution timeline, a journey roadmap, conflict-resolution, or transformation – anything that structurally resembles a narrative.

4.8. Reiterating with Repetition

Humans learn best through repetition. By consistently using the same visual cues to represent particular abstract ideas, you establish familiarity. Your viewers start to associate the visual cues with the underlying concept, thereby enhancing recall value.

4.9. Testing and Feedback

Finally, get your visuals tested by others. Fresh eyes can provide an objective perspective and spot gaps that you may have overlooked. Incorporating this feedback can make your visual communication more effective and powerful.

Comprehending abstract concepts may feel like unlocking a knotted labyrinth. However, by applying step-by-step strategies, anchored around empathy and creativity looks less of a task. So while it may initially seem like a formidable challenge, you're certainly equipped to tame the abstract beast and mold it into a visual feast! Voila, thus you have embroidered your abstract concepts intriguingly!

Chapter 5. Turning Words into Pictures

Turning words into pictures is a concept that's becoming increasingly essential in our visual world. Understanding this concept isn't just about enhancing aesthetics—it's about propelling comprehension, absorbing volumes of data swiftly, and ensuring that your messages stick.

5.1. The Essence of Visualization

Before launching into the practical aspects of converting words into images, it's vital to grasp the essence of visualization. At its core, visualization is about converting data or conceptual information into graphic form. This includes everything from flowcharts and graphs to infographics and animations. The symbolic representation helps simplify complex concepts, making them easier to comprehend.

5.2. The Why: Benefits of Visualization

Turning words into pictures bears countless benefits. These visualizations facilitate quicker absorption of information, lets you perceive trends and correlations, and can make your message more memorable and engaging.

1. Speedy Absorption: Text is sequential, forcing the reader to take in one word after the other. Visuals, on the other hand, present a chunk of information all at once, permitting quick understanding.

2. Perceiving Trends: Visuals are excellent for representing trends or patterns that may be challenging to convey in words.

Presenting data to illustrate a point often makes it more convincing.

3. Captivation: Images are more engaging than blocks of text, so using pictures or infographics can draw viewers into your content in a way that regular text might not achieve.

5.3. The How: Practical Steps to Transforming Words into Pictures

Visualizing text involves more than designing pretty graphics. It's about carefully selecting the most effective way to visually communicate your specific message. Here are a few suggestions:

1. Identify the Key Message: Start by identifying the main point you want to communicate. This will help define the elements needed in your visual.

2. Select the Correct Visual form: Not all data suits all visual forms—choose wisely to make sure your data isn't distorted or misleading. Histograms, pie charts, or line graphs might be ideal for numerical data, while a Venn diagram or flowchart could illuminate abstract concepts.

3. Design for Clarity: Pictures should clarify, not confuse. Make sure your visuals are clean, straightforward, and in sync with your overall message. Don't try to fit too much into one picture—sometimes, simple is best.

5.4. Digging Deeper: Utilizing Software Tools

There are numerous software tools available today that can aid in turning your words into pictures. Canva, for example, can serve as a powerful tool for creating infographics, diagrams, or social media images. Tableau, on the other hand, is a go-to for creating interactive data visualizations.

5.5. Translating Verbal to Visual: Common Pitfalls

While transforming words into visuals can be immensely beneficial, there are still pitfalls to dodge. The main danger is sacrificing clarity for aesthetics. Although pictures can be engaging, attractiveness should never outweigh comprehension. Always make sure your visualization conveys your message accurately.

5.6. In The End: Visualization to Connect

Finally, remember that the main aim of visualization is to connect - connect with your audience, connect complex ideas and even connect data with context. Always use visuals as a tool to make your messages clearer, more relatable and stronger in holding the attention of your audience.

Turning words into pictures is so much more than creating a pretty graphic. It's the art of transforming information into an engaging, understandable, and memorable form. Done right, these visuals will not only capture attention but will help ensure your message is not easily forgotten.

Chapter 6. Essential Tools for Visualizing Your Message

Whether you're honing a brand-new idea or clarifying existing concepts, the ability to visualize your message is an invaluable tool in your communication arsenal. Therewith, we delve into a fascinating array of tools that will assist you in making your message more visual, compelling, and memorable.

6.1. The Power of Simplicity

One of the rudiments of effective communication is simplicity. The simpler your content or the idea, the easier it is for your audience to visualize and remember.

Start by translating your complex ideas into simple, understandable elements. This could involve breaking down the idea into smaller parts or identifying the most critical aspects of the concept that your audience must understand.

By maintaining simplicity, you keep your visuals and messages uncluttered, and your audience can digest them easily. Use as few words as possible, and prioritize clarity over ornamentation. Always keep your audience and their needs in mind.

6.2. Creating Infographics

Infographics are a versatile tool that can be utilized for representing information in a visually stimulating and easily digestible manner. A well-crafted infographic can convey complex data in a more engaging manner, making it easier for your audience to understand and retain the information.

Use infographics to visualize data, explain a process, or present a timeline. Make sure to keep them clean and straightforward, emphasizing the data. A consistent color scheme and easy-to-read typography are also vital for maximizing the impact of your infographics.

6.3. Designing Compelling Presentations

Just like infographics, presentations can be an effective tool for visual communication. Broadly, a good presentation should be engaging, clear, and concise – keeping your audience's attention, delivering your message, and avoiding unnecessary details.

Use a clean design, high-quality images, and simple language. Effects such as transitions and animations should augment your content, not detract from it. Use charts, graphs, and diagrams wherever possible to replace text and simplify complex concepts.

6.4. Tools for Creating Animations

Animations can create compelling narratives by using movement to tell a story or demonstrate an idea. You can use animation tools to explain complicated concepts, guide people through a process, or create engaging promotional videos.

There are several user-friendly tools available like Powtoon, Vyond, and Animaker offering pre-designed templates and animations that you can customize for your needs. Remember that your animations should be smooth and straightforward, avoiding overly complex movements or transitions that could confuse your audience.

6.5. Harnessing the Power of Social Media

Social media provides an excellent platform to share visual content with your audience. Be it infographics, videos, or simple images with text, social media posts can be a potent tool to disseminate your message.

Make sure to tailor your visual content depending upon the platform; what works on Instagram might not work on LinkedIn. Use colors and branding consistently across platforms, ensuring your posts are easily recognizable to your audience.

6.6. Exploring Augmented and Virtual Reality

Augmented Reality (AR) and Virtual Reality (VR) provide opportunities to visualize information in innovative ways. AR overlays digital elements onto the physical world, enhancing real-life environments, while VR immerses the user in a completely virtual environment.

While these cutting-edge technologies can be quite involved, there are user-friendly tools available. These include ARKit and ARCore for AR, and tools such as Unity and Unreal Engine for VR. They enable even non-technical users to create virtual visualizations that can transform your message delivery.

6.7. Utilizing Interactive Visuals

Interactive visuals are an exciting way to engage your audience by allowing them to manipulate the information presented to them. Interactive infographics, maps, and charts can help viewers explore data at their own pace, providing a deeper understanding.

Tools like Tableau, Infogram, and Venngage allow creating interactive visuals with relative ease. It's imperative to design these visuals with the user experience in mind, ensuring the interactivity enhances the content rather than confusing the viewer.

6.8. Applying Design Principles

Regardless of the visual communication tool you are using, applying basic design principles is crucial in generating clear, beautiful, and effective visuals. Balance, contrast, emphasis, movement, pattern, rhythm, and unity should guide you in this endeavor.

Having an understanding of color theory, typography, and composition can greatly enhance the effectiveness of your visuals. Consider taking a basic design course or using design resources available online to build these skills.

The above strategies are but a subset of the vast array of visual tools you can utilize to present your message in an engaging manner. It's essential to remember that not every tool will be applicable in every scenario. You must choose wisely, keeping in mind the nature of your message, your audience's preferences, and the best way to convey your ideas effectively. Happy visualizing!

Chapter 7. Mastering the Art of Data Visualization

In an increasingly data-driven universe, the ability to condense complex narratives into clear, concrete visualizations is a skill no communicator can afford to ignore. It allows us to harness our natural inclination towards visual information and bridges the gap between abstract numbers and comprehensible insights.

7.1. Understanding The Basics Of Data Visualization

When it comes to data visualization - creativity is important but, first and foremost, the basic principles have to be well understood. Visualization is about presenting data in a graphical or pictorial form that enhances our understanding. Varieties of data visualization techniques exist - bar graphs, pie charts, scatter plots, histograms, and more complex ones like heat maps and network diagrams. The choice boils down to the nature of the data and the message you want to convey.

Creating effective visuals starts with a clear understanding of the data. What kind of data is it? What are the variables? What's the relationship between these variables? Translating these complexities intuitively in visuals will ensure that your audience grasps the information with a glance.

For instance, scatter plots are appropriate for showing relationships between variables, bar graphs for comparison between groups, and pie charts for showing parts of a whole. A wrong choice here can lead to distorted interpretations.

7.2. The Science Behind Good Design

It is one thing to turn data into a graphic. It is another to create an impactful visualization that tells a compelling story. This is where the science of the design comes in. The use of colors, shapes, size, and spacing can have profound effects on readability and understanding.

Use lighter colors to indicate less intensity and darker ones for more. Ordering data either by value or alphabetically can also help users understand the data faster. Also, consistency is key. When labeling, color-coding, or adding units to your visualization, maintain consistency. It reduces cognitive load and ensures that the users don't get confused.

7.3. Incorporating Interactivity

Interactivity harnesses the full potential of your visualization. It allows the viewers to alter some parameters to their liking, effectively engaging and captivating them more in the process. This could include filters which allow the viewers to choose what data they want to see, hover effects showing additional information, and incorporation of navigational aids like arrows.

When building interactive visualizations, be wary of overloading the users with too much information. Striking the balance between providing relevant information and maintaining a clean and non-cluttered design is essential for preserving the impact of your visualization.

7.4. Tools For Data Visualization

In the digital age, myriad tools are at your disposal for turning your data into engaging visuals.

Tableau is a popular one. While it is highly sophisticated, its in-built tutorials make it user-friendly. Another is D3.js, a JavaScript library that provides advanced flexibility. For designers just starting out, Microsoft Excel, Google Sheets, or Canva can suffice.

What's vital to remember as you pick your tool is that the ultimate aim remains to create a storytelling visualization. Therefore, consider what kind of design suits your narrative best before you choose.

7.5. Building Your First Visualization

Let's put theory into practice and construct your first visualization. Suppose you are tasked with visualizing a company's sales over the previous years.

Firstly, understand the data. You have to know the years the data spans and the pertinent changes that occurred over time. Next, depending upon what you want your audience to focus on, choose a suitable chart. For this case, a line chart showing the trend over time would be appropriate.

Then design the chart. You can use Excel for this purpose. Fill the data in your cells, highlighting the column with the data entries and choosing the 'Insert Line Chart' option. Be sure to label your chart and axes. Make sure the line is thick enough for easy view.

In conclusion, mastering the art of data visualization can significantly elevate your communication skills. It's all about understanding the information you want to express, choosing the proper design, and using the right tool to do so. Remember, the ultimate goal is to ensure your audience receives the message as seamlessly as possible. With practice and the pointers provided above, the path to captivating data visualization beckons. Let's embark on this insightful journey of turning data to visual masterpieces.

Chapter 8. The Role of Colors in Expressing Meaning

The world is not black and white, literally and metaphorically. We live in a universe teeming with hues - each carrying distinct connotations that tickle different emotional chords. From stop signs to the regalia on national flags, or the soothing design of a company's logo, colors play an integral part of human cognition and behavior.

8.1. The Psychological Impact of Colors

The symbolism and impact of colors reach back into ancient past. Various civilizations associated different colors with their deities, essential life elements or potent cultural symbols. In the modern world, these colors have found a new arena to express their influence: visual communication.

For instance, fast-food restaurants often adorn their logos and venues with reds and yellows, subtly inciting hunger and speed - elements that align with their business model. On the contrary, healthcare providers and counselors leverage blues and greens to convey a sense of calm and caring.

Evidently, the conscious use of colors can enhance the efficacy of your message, consciously and subconsciously affecting the viewer's perceptions.

8.2. Assignment of Meaning to Colors

The attribution of meaning to colors is largely cultural and varies across different societies. However, certain universal associations do exist.

Red, for example, often symbolizes energy, passion, and danger. But it can also represent love and excitement. Yellow, the color of the sun, symbolizes warmth, happiness, and optimism, but can also represent caution.

Green, being the color of nature, is often associated with growth, serenity, and fertility, but it can also signify jealousy or inexperience. Blue, the color of the sky and the sea, is associated with peace, tranquility, and loyalty, but ironically, it's also linked to sadness.

8.3. The Use of Colors in Branding

In the context of branding and marketing, the colors chosen as part of a logo or design can significantly impact how the audience perceives the brand. McDonald's, for instance, uses red and yellow, which inspire feelings of energy, excitement, and hunger. Twitter, on the other hand, employs a lighter, calming shade of blue, resonating with its purpose to facilitate serene communication.

Success in branding requires the perception created by colors to align with the core values of your business or the message you intend to convey. Thus, understanding the different cultural and emotional impacts of colors becomes an essential part of effective communication.

8.4. Colors and Data Visualization

Similarly, colors play a critical role in data visualization, where the appropriate use of colors can make graphs and charts significantly more comprehensible. For example, if you're creating a heatmap, warmer colors (such as red and orange) generally represent greater values or higher concentration and cooler colors (such as blue and green), the opposite.

However, making informed decisions in the use of colors can avert potential confusion; using a rainbow color palette, for example, can lead to misinterpretation of data due to the non-linear perception of colors by the human eye.

8.5. In Conclusion

While the power and influence of colors in visual communication are immense, they must be used with caution and research. It is crucial to remember that colors may have different connotations in different cultures. Therefore, understanding the target audience's cultural background can significantly sway perception. Thus, in any form of visual communication, colors truly are the subtle narrators intricating their hue-tinted tales. Be it an illustrious infographic, a beguiling brand logo, or a simple social media post, effective use of colors can punctuate your message with an amplified emotional response.

Chapter 9. Creating Compelling Presentation Slides

Successful slide creation is no accident. To effectively communicate your message and engage your audience, each element of the slide - from the background color to the font size - must be carefully chosen for the best possible effect.

Let us start our journey towards creating compelling presentation slides.

9.1. Understanding Your Audience

Before designing your presentation, understand who your audience is. Are you speaking to senior management within your company or presenting to a diverse group at a conference? Perhaps you're delivering a sales pitch to a prospective client. Your audience's preferences, familiarity with the topic, and expectations significantly influence your slide design.

1. **Assessing Knowledge and Interest:** If your audience is familiar with the topic, avoid basic explanations. Instead, focus on new insights or applications. Conversely, if the subject is new to them, you'll need to start with the basics and progress at a comfortable pace.

2. **Determining Presentation Setting:** A presentation in a small meeting room might permit more text and details, while a large conference setting demands bolder, simpler slides to ensure legibility.

3. **Addressing Cultural Differences:** If you're addressing a diverse audience, be mindful of cultural interpretations of colors,

symbols, and images since they can sway perceptions of your message.

9.2. Planning Your Story

Every presentation should tell a story that brings your audience on a journey. Hence, ensure your slides connect to build a coherent narrative.

1. **Introducing the Topic:** Begin the presentation by setting the context, providing a broad overview.

2. **Main Theme and Subthemes:** Identify your main theme and all subthemes. Each should correspond to a section of your presentation.

3. **Flow and Transition:** Make sure the transition from one slide to another is smooth and logical. Use signposts to show progression or to emphasize a shift in thinking.

9.3. Designing the Slides

It's at the intersection of content and design where the magic happens. While your content carries the story, design has the power to enhance it.

1. **Slide Layout:** Consistency in slide layout reduces cognitive load. Limit text on each slide. Instead, use bullet points or short sentences. Stick to one or two main points per slide.

2. **Visuals:** Graphs, charts, diagrams, and pictures can express complex concepts succinctly and compellingly. However, use them wisely and judiciously.

3. **Fonts and Colors:** Choose fonts and colors that reflect your message well and are easy on the eyes. Use contrast to your advantage.

9.4. Integrating Multimedia

Multimedia elements add a new dimension to your slides and create a more engaging experience for the audience.

1. **Video Clips:** Short video clips can illustrate complex points, garner interest, or introduce humor to lighten the mood.

2. **Audio Clips:** Audio can be particularly helpful in setting the context, stirring emotional responses, or varying the presentation pace.

3. **Animations:** Used sparingly and sensibly, animations can highlight key points or show relationships between concepts.

9.5. Delivering the Presentation

Even the most well-designed slides can fall flat if not effectively presented.

1. **Presenter Notes:** Your slides should serve as cues. Use presenter notes to expand on the points on the screen.

2. **Presentation Style:** Engage your audience with your enthusiasm and passion. Vary your tone and pace to maintain interest.

3. **Handling Questions:** Anticipate questions and incorporate potential answers within your slides, effectively using them as a tool during Q&A sessions.

Creating compelling slides requires deliberate thought, good design, and a clear understanding of your audience and your message. It is an art that requires practice, but with these tips in your toolkit, you can craft slides that will engage your audience, effectively communicate your message, and ensure your content stands out. With patience and practice, you will mould from this clay of ideas a masterpiece of communication.

Chapter 10. Visual Communication in Social Media

Our journey begins in a domain that has revolutionized our global interactions in exponential ways - social media. Navigating the visual communication landscape here is crucial, mainly because 3.6 billion people depend on it daily. Whether you're an individual hoping to maintain human connections, a startup striving for visibility, or a multinational company aiming to reinforce brand loyalty, visual communication on social media bridges the gap between information and understanding, strategy and success.

10.1. The Importance of Visual Media In Social Media Communication

Social Media platforms are intrinsically designed to engage users, keeping them coming back for more. The kingpin of this engagement - visual content. Tweets with images receive 150% more retweets than their lowly counterparts without images. Facebook posts with images see 2.3 times more engagement than those without. A smart interchange of images, videos, GIFs, memes, and infographics can be a game-changer in maintaining and increasing your audience's short attention span. It aids comprehension, improves retention, and provokes emotion - driving sharing and discussion within users' networks, significantly contributing to virality.

10.2. Understanding The Visual Styles Across Different Platforms

The next step in our journey is to comprehend the varied visual styles of different platforms. Instagram is a quick, colorful scroll with captivating images that catch the eye and create a story. Pinterest, the mood board of the internet, elicits feelings of desire and aspiration. Twitter allows the wittiest of minds to go wild but often asks for bite-sized takeaways with compelling visuals. Coupled with understanding your audience demographics, mastering the unique visual nuances can significantly increase engagement rates.

10.3. Stirring Emotions through Visuals

A fascinating aspect of visual communication is its power to evoke emotions. Colors, for example, can influence how we feel and react. Blue can instill trust, green renewal, and red excitement. Leveraging the psychology of color in your visual content can impact user engagement. Similarly, the strategic use of shapes, lines, and spaces can stir emotions or provide context. Remember, both the rational and emotional aspects play crucial roles in decision-making processes, especially when it comes to sharing, commenting, or buying.

10.4. The Magic of Infographics

There's something almost magical about turning complex textual information into easily digestible graphics - infographics. Reading an infographic is like seeing the story unfold right before your eyes. In fact, infographics are liked and shared on social media three times more than any other type of content. Crafting clear, engaging, and effective infographics require consideration of color schemes, typography, layouts, and icons that resonate with your branding and your audience.

10.5. Creating a Consistent Visual Brand Identity

Consistency is key when creating a visual brand identity on social media. A consistent theme in terms of colors, text, and imagery can accentuate your brand and make it familiar and identifiable. When people see visuals that adhere to a specific design guideline, they are more likely to associate them with your brand. This allows you to build a robust digital presence, enhancing the conversion rates significantly.

10.6. Short Videos and Live Feeds

Thanks to the surge in internet speeds and user attention spans, social media users are more inclined towards interactive content, increasing the importance of short videos and live feeds. They allow you to put your brand in motion, giving you the power to control the narrative truly. Engaging videos not only grab viewers' attention but also increase message retention rates.

10.7. The Power of User Generated Content

Another way to amplify your visual communication strategy on social media is by leveraging user-generated content (UGC). Acknowledging and sharing customer's posts involving your product or service not only provides authentic, relatable visuals but also increases trust and cultivates brand loyalty among your audience.

10.8. Analytics: Measuring Your Impact

Finally, no strategy is complete without measuring its impact. Social media platforms offer in-depth integrated analytics to help you evaluate your visual communication strategy. Track how your posts perform over time, see how people engage with different types of content, and make data-driven decisions to craft your future approach.

In conclusion, visual communication on social media is not just about posting attractive media. It requires thought, understanding, planning, execution, and constant analysis. With the strategies stated above, you can create a visual communication style that resonates with your target audience and achieves your desired goals. Remember, visual communication is a language. When utilized correctly, it will allow you to weave compelling narratives that engage, inform, and inspire.

Chapter 11. Evaluating the Effectiveness of Your Visual Message

Every model of communication must ultimately answer the same critical question: is the message getting across in the way you intended? A beautiful presentation or a compelling infographic may wow your audience at first glance, but if it doesn't accurately and effectively communicate the desired information, its beauty is in vain. The evaluation of the effectiveness of your visual message is essential to creating meaningful communication.

11.1. The Importance of Evaluating Your Visual Messages

Evaluation is the vital final step in the process of creating a visual message. It provides a critical opportunity to step back, assess, and revise. By evaluating your visual message, you can identify areas of improvement, eliminate misunderstandings, and refine your message to ensure a better communication experience the next time. It keeps you in sync with your target audience by making sure your message resonates with them and their perception.

11.2. Criteria for Evaluating Your Visual Message

There are multiple factors to consider when evaluating the effectiveness of your visual message. Review your work in terms of clarity, simplicity, consistency, accuracy, and viewer understanding.

- Clarity: Does your image clearly express your message? Is it easily understandable, or is it complex and confusing?

- Simplicity: Have you used simple, easy-to-understand visuals that complement your message rather than confuse it?

- Consistency: Is your visual style consistent throughout your message? Consistency can considerably enhance viewer comprehension.

- Accuracy: Does your visual accurately convey the message you want your audience to receive?

- Viewer understanding: Have you considered your audience's familiarity with your subject matter? Have you provided enough context for them to grasp your visual message?

11.3. Techniques for Testing Your Visual Messages

Two widely used methods to empirically test the effectiveness of your visual message are Direct Feedback and A/B Testing.

- Direct Feedback: Direct feedback involves presenting your visual message to a select group and gathering their reactions to it. Encourage your sample audience to be brutally honest in their assessments. Gather feedback on the clarity, design, and overall effectiveness of the visual message. Use this feedback to refine and improve your visuals.

- A/B Testing: In an A/B test, you create two versions of your visual and present them to two different test groups. Each version has only one variable change (such as a different color scheme or the addition of a data table), allowing you to pinpoint the effect of a specific change on your message's effectiveness.

11.4. Addressing Negative Feedback

Conceiving and creating a visual message is a course filled with trials and errors. There can be feedback indicating that your message is not as effective as you assumed. Evaluation allows you to rectify these issues.

Negative feedback may seem disheartening, but it's crucially productive. If a viewer is confused by a graphic, try simplifying it. If the response is far from what was intended, consider adding more explicative elements. Slight tweaks can make world-transforming changes in the effectiveness of your visual message.

11.5. The Iterative Process: Assess, Refine, Assess Again

Understand that evaluating your visual message isn't a one-off process. Creating the perfect visual message is recursive; it involves incessant adjustments and improvements. Experiment with different approaches, analyze the responses, and adjust accordingly. Remember, the ultimate objective is to create an impactful and understandable visual message that resonantly communicates your information.

11.6. The Broader Impact

Think beyond the immediate response to your visual message. Reflect on whether your visuals contribute to shaping the overall narrative you have visualized for your brand or your message. The effectiveness of individual pieces of visual communication feeds into broader narratives and conversations.

Evaluation is the key to improving your visual messages. It sheds light on your message's weaknesses and opens pathways to improve them, thus facilitating more effective communication. Remember, every feedback is your stepping stone to creating clearer, more impactful visual messages. Don't shirk the hard truths; instead, embrace them and learn from them to build a visual legacy that stands the test of time!